Jungle
Animals

Series Editor Deborah Lock
Editor Arpita Nath
Senior Art Editor Ann Cannings
Art Editor Yamini Panwar
Senior Producer, Pre-production Nikoleta Parasaki
Picture Researcher Sakshi Saluja
Jacket Designer Charlotte Jennings
DTP Designers Ashok Kumar and Dheeraj Singh
Managing Editor Soma B. Chowdhury
Managing Art Editor Ahlawat Gunjan
Art Director Martin Wilson

Reading Consultant
Linda Gambrell, Ph.D.

First published in Great Britain in 2016
by Dorling Kindersley Limited
80 Strand, London, WC2R 0RL

A CIP catalogue record for this book
is available from the British Library
ISBN: 978-0-2412-2513-4

Printed and bound in China.

The publisher would like to thank the following for their kind permission to reproduce their photographs:
(Key: a=above, b=below/bottom, c=center, l=left, r=right, t=top)
1 Getty Images: Anup Shah. **4 Dorling Kindersley:** Whipsnade Zoo, Bedfordshire (cra). 5 Philip Dowell: (crb).
Dreamstime.com: Eric Isselee (cl). **Science Photo Library:** John Mitchell (tc). **6 naturepl.com:** Jack Dykinga (bl).
6–7 Corbis: Jim Zuckerman. **8–9 naturepl.com:** Roland Seitre. **10–11 Corbis:** DLILLC. **12–13 Corbis:** Kevin Kurek/dpa.
14-15 naturepl.com: Pete Oxford. **16-17 Alamy Images:** Design Pics Inc. **18-19 Getty Images:** heatherwest. **19 Robert
Harding Picture Library:** Frans Lanting (c). **20-21 Getty Images:** Clara Zamith. **22 Alamy Images:** Design Pics Inc (bl);
Arco Images GmbH (cla). **Dreamstime.com:** Eric Isselee (clb); Rinus Baak (cl). **24 naturepl.com:** Jack Dykinga (bl).
Endpapers: **Dorling Kindersley:** Frank Greenaway. **Jacket credits:** *Front:* **Getty:** Heather West (c), Andy Rouse (tc). **dk.com:**
Jerry Young (cl). *Back:* **dk.com:** Dave King, Courtesy of Whipsnade Zoo, Bedfordshire (tl)

All other images © Dorling Kindersley
For further information see: www.dkimages.com

A WORLD OF IDEAS:
SEE ALL THERE IS TO KNOW

www.dk.com

Contents

Enter the jungle,
if you dare!
Look up! Look down!
Look out!

Parrots

A parrot flies
over the jungle.
Its feathers flash red,
yellow, green and blue.

feathers

Toucans

beak

berry

A toucan picks
a berry with
its large, long beak.

Orangutans

Orangutans swing from tree to tree. They move very quickly.

Sun Bears

Sun bears climb
the trees.
Their long claws
grip the branches.

claw

# Giant Anteaters

snout

An anteater sniffs
an ants' nest
with its long snout.

ants' nest

Tarantulas

ground

A tarantula feels
the ground shake
with its hairy legs.

hairy legs

Tigers

A tiger hides
in the grass.
It watches and waits,
ready to leap.

Jaguars

A jaguar rests.
Ssh!
Quiet in the jungle,
please!

Glossary

Beak
hard, pointed
bird's mouth

Claws
sharp, curved
toe-points

Feathers
soft covering
on a bird's body

Snout
long, pointed nose
and mouth used
to smell and eat

Spider's legs
hairy body parts
used to move and
sense animals nearby

Index

A Note to Parents

DK Readers is a four-level interactive reading adventure series for children, developing the habit of reading widely for both pleasure and information.

Beautiful illustrations and superb full-colour photographs combine with engaging, easy-to-read narratives to offer a fresh approach to each subject in the series. Each DK Reader is guaranteed to capture a child's interest while developing his or her reading skills, general knowledge and love of reading.

The four levels of DK Readers are aimed at different reading abilities, enabling you to choose the books that are exactly right for your child:

Level 1: Learning to read
Level 2: Beginning to read
Level 3: Beginning to read alone
Level 4: Reading alone

The "normal" age at which a child begins to read can be anywhere from three to eight years old. Adult participation through the lower levels is very helpful for providing encouragement, discussing storylines and sounding out unfamiliar words.

No matter which level you select, you can be sure that you are helping your child learn to read, then read to learn!

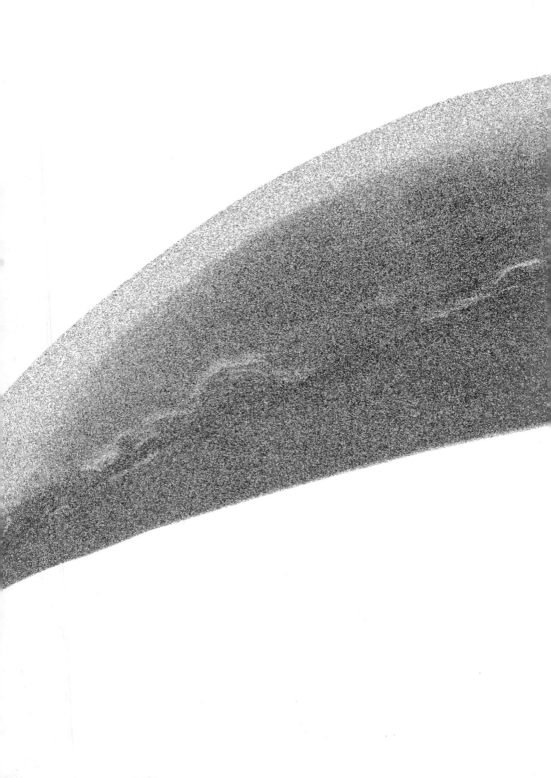